KNOWABOUT

Numbers

KNOWABOUT

Numbers

Text: Henry Pluckrose
Photography: Chris Fairclough

Franklin Watts
London/New York/Sydney/Toronto

© 1988 Franklin Watts

First published in Great Britain by

Franklin Watts
12a Golden Square
London W1

First published in the USA by

Franklin Watts Inc
387 Park Avenue South
New York 10016

ISBN: UK edition 0 86313 507 2

ISBN: US edition 0–531–10453–2
Library of Congress
Catalog Card No: 87–50588

Editor: Ruth Thomson
Design: Edward Kinsey

Typesetting: Keyspools Ltd
Printed in Hong Kong

About this book

This book is designed for use in the home, playgroup, and infant school.

Mathematics is part of the child's world. It is not just about interpreting numbers or in mastering the tricks of addition or multiplication. Mathematics is about *Ideas*. These ideas (or concepts) have been developed over the centuries to help explain particular qualities, such as size, weight, height, as well as relationships and comparisons. Yet all too often the important part which an understanding of mathematics will play in a child's development is forgotten or ignored.

Most adults can solve simple mathematical tasks by "doing them in their head." For example you can probably add up or subtract simple numbers without the need for counters, beads or fingers. Young children find such abstractions almost impossible to master. They need to see, talk, touch and experiment.

The photographs in this book and the text which supports them have been prepared with one major aim. They have been chosen to encourage talk around topics which are essentially mathematical. By talking with you, the young reader will be helped to explore some of the central concepts which underpin mathematics. It is upon an understanding of these concepts that a child's future mastery of mathematics will be built.

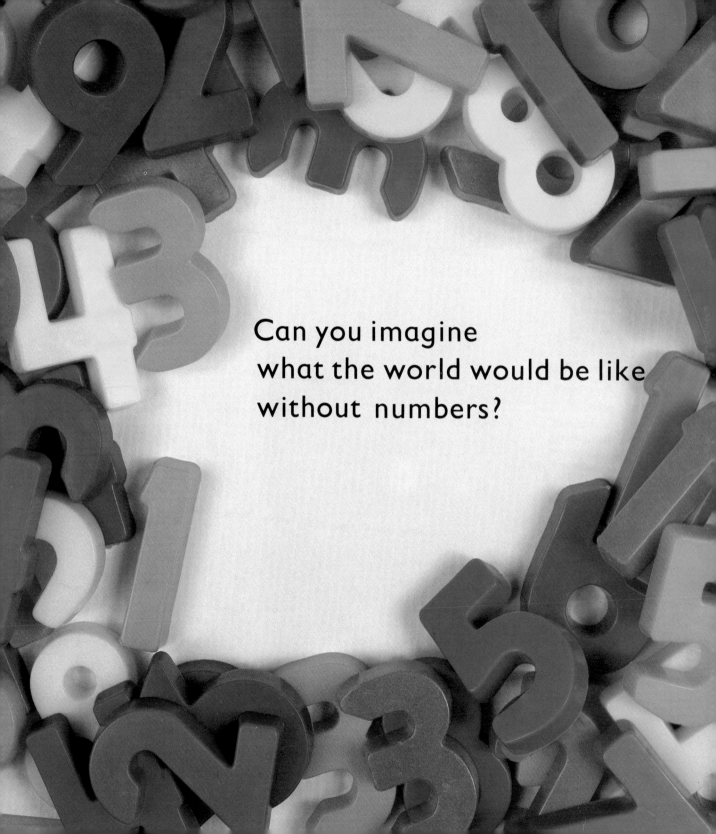

Can you imagine
what the world would be like
without numbers?

3

OUVERT
9ʰ A 11ʰ30 - 14ʰ A 18ʰ.
LE SAMEDI DE 9ʰ A 11ʰ

There are
numbers
all around us.

There are
numbers
on doors . . .

on cars. . . . .

74 BAYOU STATE 75
145 I 073
EXPIRES
MAR 31
LOUISIANA
LOUISIANA
LOUISIANA
MAR 85
12375930

on telephones . . .

and money.

Numbers help us in many ways.

This is a road number. How does it help drivers

This streetcar
has a route number.
How does this help
passengers?

What do the numbers on these bottles tell you?

These shoes
have a number
printed inside.
What do the numbers
tell you?

Months are counted in days.
Each day has a number.

1	2	3	4	5
6	7	8	9	10	11	12
13	14	15	16	17	18	19
20	21	22	23	24	25	26
27	28	29	30	31		

What is the date today?
Do you know the date of your birthday?

What number
will you have
on your next birthday cake?

Numbers are useful
for measuring.

We use them to measure time . . .

speed . . .

and heat.

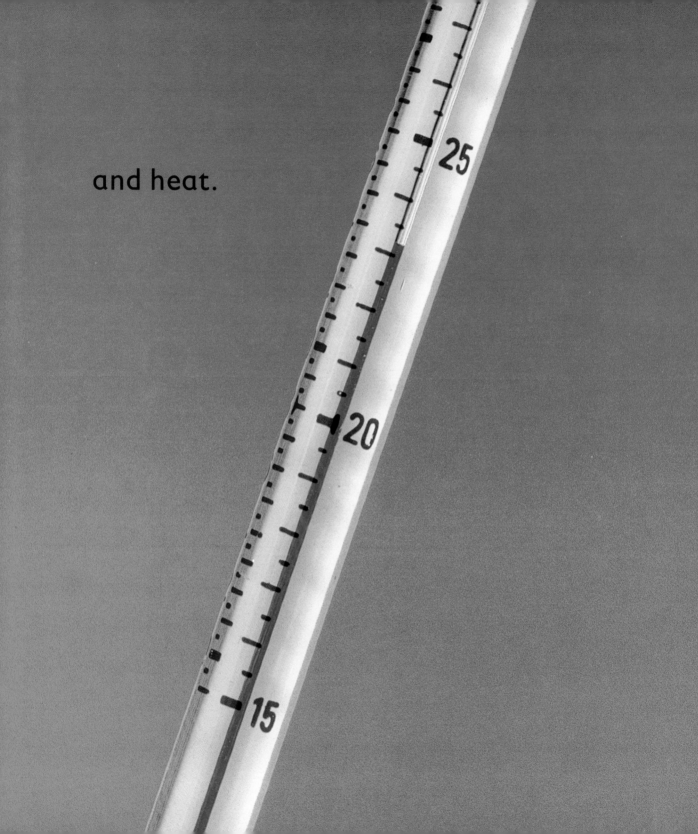

Why does
an elevator
have numbers?

Which one
would you press
to go to
the third floor?

We use them
to measure

height . . .

and length.

We use them to measure weight . . .

and liquids.

MILLILITRES

½ LITRE — 500

— 400

— 300

¼ LITRE — 250

— 200

APPROX. MEASURES

— 100

People in races are often given
a number to identify them.

Which car is leading in this race?

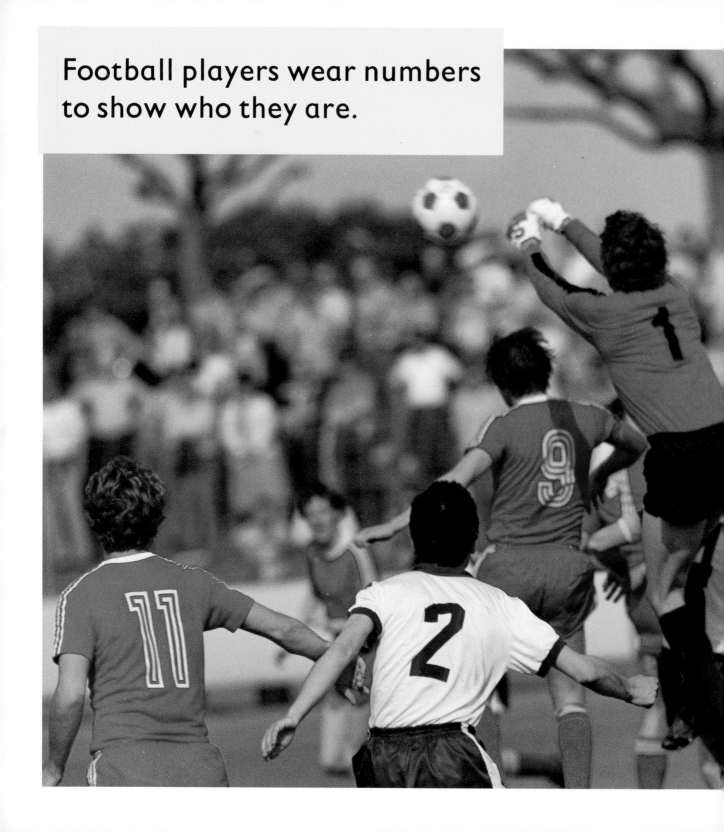

Football players wear numbers
to show who they are.

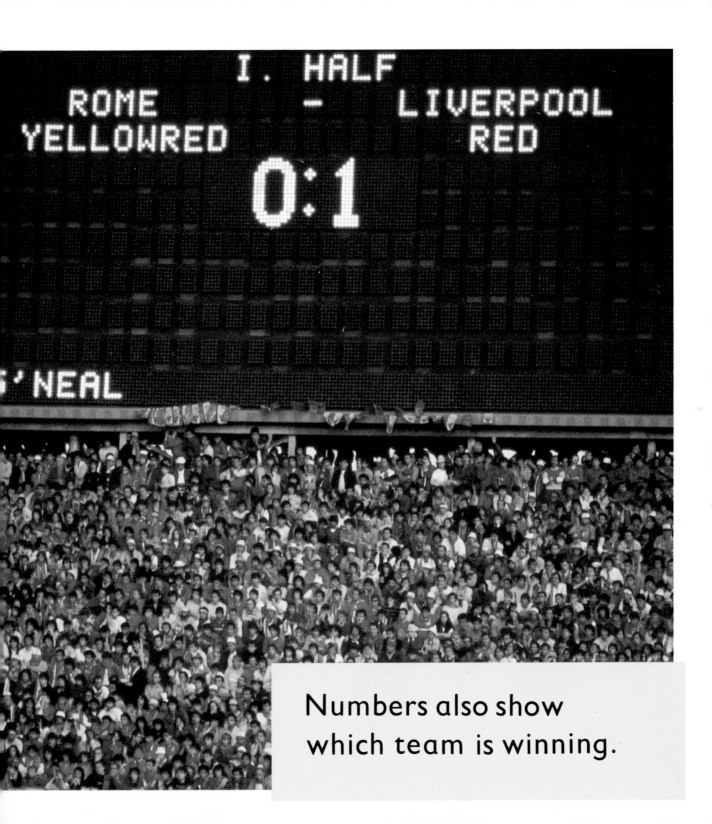

I. HALF
ROME — LIVERPOOL
YELLOWRED RED
0:1

'NEAL

Numbers also show which team is winning.

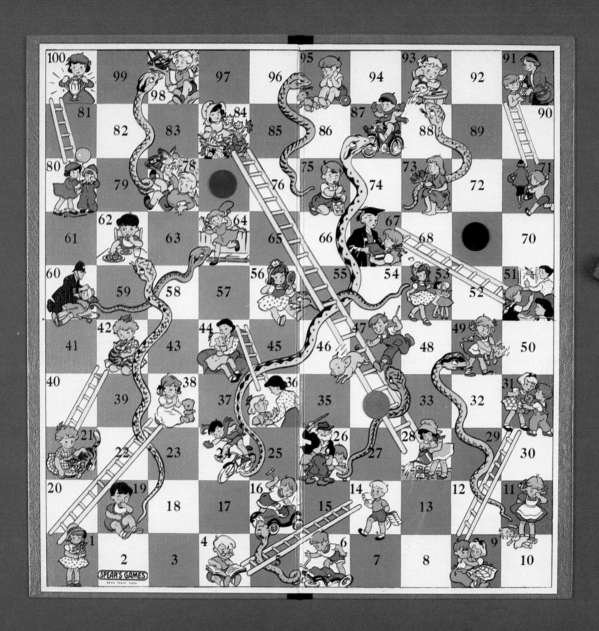

You can play games using numbers.
Do you know how to play this game . . . . .

or this one?

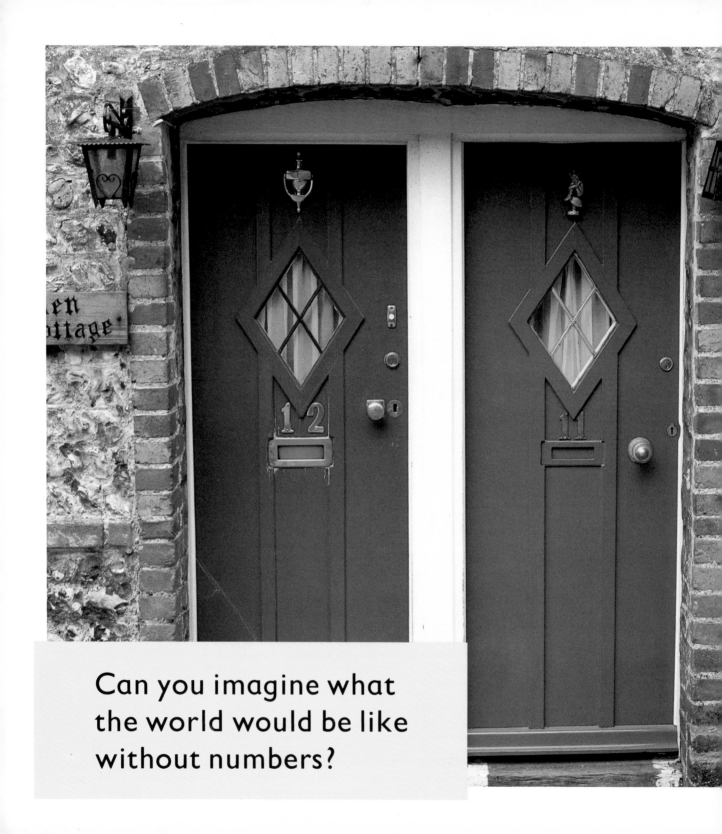

Can you imagine what the world would be like without numbers?